Dear Parent:

Your child's love of reading s  T0253429

Every child learns to read in a different way and at his or her own speed. Some go back and forth between reading levels and read favorite books again and again. Others read through each level in order. You can help your young reader improve and become more confident by encouraging his or her own interests and abilities. From books your child reads with you to the first books he or she reads alone, there are I Can Read Books for every stage of reading:

SHARED READING
Basic language, word repetition, and whimsical illustrations, ideal for sharing with your emergent reader

BEGINNING READING
Short sentences, familiar words, and simple concepts for children eager to read on their own

READING WITH HELP
Engaging stories, longer sentences, and language play for developing readers

READING ALONE
Complex plots, challenging vocabulary, and high-interest topics for the independent reader

I Can Read Books have introduced children to the joy of reading since 1957. Featuring award-winning authors and illustrators and a fabulous cast of beloved characters, I Can Read Books set the standard for beginning readers.

A lifetime of discovery begins with the magical words **"I Can Read!"**

*Visit www.icanread.com for information
on enriching your child's reading experience.*

**Visit www.zonderkidz.com/icanread for more faith-based
I Can Read! titles from Zonderkidz.**

God saw everything he had made.
And it was very good.
—*Genesis 1:31*

ZONDERKIDZ

Adam and Eve in the Garden
Copyright © 2008 by Zondervan
Illustrations © by Zondervan

An **I Can Read Book**

Requests for information should be addressed to:
Zonderkidz, 3900 *Sparks Drive SE, Grand Rapids, Michigan 49546*

Library of Congress Cataloging-in-Publication Data
    Adam and Eve in the garden : my first I can read! / illustrated by Kelly Pulley.
       p. cm.
    Includes bibliographical references and index.
    ISBN 978-0-310-71552-8 (softcover : alk. paper)
    1. Adam (Biblical figure)—Juvenile literature. 2. Eve (Biblical figure)—Juvenile literature. 3. Eden—Juvenile
literature. 4. Bible stories,
       English—O.T. Genesis. I. Pulley, Kelly.
    BS580.A4A324 2008
    222'.1109505—dc22

             2007012119

Editor: Kristen Tuinstra
Art Direction: Jody Langley
Cover Design: Sarah Molegraaf

Adam and Eve in the Garden

pictures by Kelly Pulley

In the beginning,
the world was empty.
But God had a plan.

"I will make
many good things,"
God said.

On day one God said,
"I will make day and night."
So he did.

On day two God split
the water from the air.
He said, "Here are the sky
and the sea."

God made land on day three.
Plants grew on the land.
Fruit trees grew there too.

On day four God put the sun
and the moon in the sky.

On day five
God made birds
to fly in the sky.

He made fish to swim
in the ocean.

Day six was busy too.
God made the rest
of the animals.

Then God made the first man.

God named him Adam.

God loved Adam.

God rested on day seven.

He was so happy!

Adam was happy too.

God put Adam in a garden.

The garden was called Eden.

Adam took care of Eden.

He took care of the animals.

He even named all the animals.
"You will be called a 'parrot.'
You will be called a 'butterfly.'"

One day God made Eve.
She helped Adam take care of
the garden and the animals.

God gave Adam and Eve one rule.
God said, "Do not eat
fruit from this tree."

Later, a sneaky snake
was in the tree.

"Eve, you can eat this fruit.
It is fine!" the snake said.

Eve ate the fruit.

Then Adam ate the fruit too.

God was sad.

They had broken his one rule.

This was called a "sin."

"Eve gave me the fruit,"
Adam said.

"Snake tricked me," Eve said.

God said, "Snake,
you must move on your
belly and eat dust."

God told Adam and Eve,
"You must leave.
You did not follow my rule."

Adam and Eve left the garden.
They were very sad.

But God would always love them.

He made another plan.

One day, God would send Jesus.
Jesus would save everyone
from their sins.

Milton Keynes UK
Ingram Content Group UK Ltd.
UKHW022001291024
450273UK00006B/69